Novel Ideas Classic

Lord of the Flies
William Golding

Writers and Editors of Novel Ideas Classic

Mark Angney
Editorial Consultant

Elizabeth Alexander
Education Consultant

Jane M. Archibald
Education Consultant

Richard Barbieri
*Co-Director, Writing Institute
Milton Academy*

Sidney J. Black
*Chairman, Department of
Humanities, Boston University*

Lillian A. Buckley
Education Consultant

Claire M. Daniel
Education Consultant

Beth G. Davis
Education Consultant

Kathryn M. Faucher
Education Consultant

Audrey Friedman
*Adjunct Professor of Education
Boston College*

Joan Friedman
Language Arts Teacher

Roon Frost
Education Consultant

Donald Gallo
Professor of English

Maxine G. Glassman
High School English Teacher

Stephanie K. Johnson
Education Consultant

**Edward Lawrence
Katzenbach**
Education Consultant

Gwendolyn Kerr
Education Consultant

Richard Lederer
Writer

Barbara Matthews
Education Consultant

James E. McDermott
Education Consultant

Patricia M. Mote
Education Consultant

Bren Price
Education Consultant

Bonita Rettman
Education Consultant

John Savage
*Professor of Reading
Boston College*

Owen Shows
Education Consultant

Myka-Lynn Sokoloff
Education Consultant

David M. Smith
*English Department Chairman
Milton Academy*

Copyright © 1997 Sundance Publishing, 234 Taylor Street, Littleton, MA 01460
All rights reserved.

Tree and typewriter images Copyright © 1997 Photodisc, Inc.
ISBN 0-94014-621-5
10 9 8 7 6 5 4 3 2 1 DSV

Table of Contents

The Teacher's Guide

Introduction to Novel Ideas Classic	4
Teaching Objectives	4
Using Novel Ideas Classic in Your Classroom	5
Using Literature to Teach Skills	6
Synopsis of *Lord of the Flies*	8
About the Author	9
Socratic Discussion of *Lord of the Flies*	10
Writing Activities	11
Integrating Language Arts	12
Integrating the Curriculum	13
More Books to Read	13
Teaching Strategies	14
Additional Teaching Strategy Suggestions	19
Answer Key	51

Student Reproducible Activity Sheets

1 Word Meaning: Leadership
Critical-Creative Thinking
Prereading
LEVEL 2

2 Reading Guide: Chapters 1–3
Reading Comprehension/Critical-Creative Thinking
Prereading
LEVEL 2

3 Characterization
Critical Thinking
After Chapter 3
LEVEL 2

4 Cause and Effect (Literal)
Reading Comprehension
After Chapter 3
LEVEL 1

5 Characterization (Literal/Inferential)
Literary Analysis
During Chapters 1–3
LEVEL 2

6 Cause and Effect (Critical)
Reading Comprehension
After Chapter 3
LEVEL 2

7 Reading Guide: Chapters 4–6
Reading Comprehension/Critical-Creative Thinking
After Chapter 3
LEVEL 2

8 Point of View
Literary Analysis
After Chapter 4
LEVEL 3

9 Mood
Written Language
After Chapter 5
LEVEL 2

10 Characterization (Inferential)
Literary Analysis
After Chapter 5
LEVEL 2

11 Words in Context
Vocabulary
After Chapter 6
LEVEL 2

Novel Ideas Classic

12 Critical Reading
Reading Comprehension
After Chapter 6
LEVEL 3

13 Reading Guide: Chapters 7–9
Reading Comprehension/Critical-Creative Thinking
After Chapter 6
LEVEL 2

14 Cause and Effect (Inferential)
Reading Comprehension/Inferential Thinking
After Chapter 9
LEVEL 2

15 Sequence of Events (Literal)
Reading Comprehension
After Chapter 9
LEVEL 1

16 Theme (Literal)
Literary Analysis
After Chapter 9
LEVEL 1

17 Critical Reading
Reading Comprehension
After Chapter 9
LEVEL 3

18 Reading Guide: Chapters 10–12
Reading Comprehension/Critical-Creative Thinking
After Chapter 9
LEVEL 2

19 Antonyms
Vocabulary
After Chapter 11
LEVEL 2

20 Structural Analysis
Vocabulary
After Chapter 12
LEVEL 2

21 Theme
Literary Analysis
After Chapter 12
LEVEL 3

22 Word Meaning
Vocabulary
After Chapter 12
LEVEL 3

23 Sequence
Reading Comprehension
After Chapter 12
LEVEL 1

24 Theme
Literary Analysis
After Chapter 12
LEVEL 2

25 Characterization (Inferential/Critical)
Literary Analysis
After Chapter 12
LEVEL 3

26 Characterization (Inferential/Critical)
Literary Analysis
After Chapter 12
LEVEL 3

Tests for Student Assessment

1 Vocabulary
Vocabulary
After Chapter 12
LEVEL 2

2 Characters
Literary Analysis
After Chapter 12
LEVEL 2

3 Facts/Ideas
Reading Comprehension
After Chapter 12
LEVEL 2

4 Facts/Ideas
Reading Comprehension
After Chapter 12
LEVEL 2

5 Essays
Writing
After Chapter 12
LEVEL 2

Introduction to Novel Ideas Classic

Why Teach Literature?

We teach literature because literature provides students with experiences about people, places, ideas, and language that students can rarely, if ever, obtain in other ways. The full-length novel or play allows its reader to enter wholeheartedly into the life of another person—adult or adolescent, rich or poor, near or distant. Through a Huck Finn or a Holden Caulfield, students can explore their own youth; or they can experience the varieties of adult life, from the failed success of Jay Gatsby to the noble defeat of Winston Smith.

Novels offer insight into other worlds at different times. Students can experience imaginative re-creations of the past, such as *A Tale of Two Cities,* or prophetic visions of the future, as in *Fahrenheit 451*. Books such as *The Chocolate War* or *Of Mice and Men* reveal our own and other Americas, while *Hiroshima* and *The Old Man and the Sea* expose us to other cultures and other ways of living and dying.

Fiction introduces students to a range of problems, from the special ones of their youth to the universal ones of humanity, and shows students how to deal with them. Students can stretch their abilities to follow the intricacies of a complex plot or a large cast of characters. They can explore an idea—prejudice, love, war—in depth and from many different vantage points.

Experiencing a prolonged encounter with a single writer's style helps young people to see how each artist finds a distinctive voice to express a unique vision of the world. Perhaps this can help students to choose a voice or a vision for themselves.

How can I teach literature when I have so many students who lack basic skills?

Grouping students of different levels of ability into smaller heterogeneous groups allows students an opportunity to decipher the material's language or comprehend its meaning. Then all levels of students can not only enjoy the reading process but also develop basic skills, expand vocabulary, and give attention to their own writing in the context of a longer work. Novel Ideas Classic Resource Books can answer the multiple needs of students at all levels of ability.

Objectives of this Resource Book

To help students

- build vocabularies based on the language used in the novel.
- develop the reading comprehension skills of recognizing sequence of events and determining cause and effect relationships.
- develop the literary analysis skills of recognizing theme and understanding characterization.
- practice writing skills or writing to create a mood.

Using Novel Ideas Classic in Your Classroom

Novel Ideas Classic provides
- a series of individualized exercises that can be used with students at different ability levels.
- activities that include reading comprehension, literary analysis, vocabulary building, writing, speaking, viewing, and listening.

Each Novel Ideas Classic Resource Book contains three parts:
- a Teacher's Guide
- a set of twenty-six Activity Sheets
- a set of five Tests for Student Assessment

The Teacher's Guide
- gives suggestions for introducing the novel and for supplementing the text with additional reading, writing, oral, and artistic activities.
- describes teaching strategies for using the Activity Sheets in teaching the book.
- includes a rationale for teaching the specific text, a synopsis of the book, and information about the author or the era in which the story takes place.

The Activity Sheets
The Activity Sheets are indexed by
- skill area (vocabulary, reading comprehension, literary analysis, and writing activities).
- level of difficulty (LEVEL 1, less demanding; LEVEL 2, average difficulty; LEVEL 3, more challenging).
- appropriate location in the teaching sequence (before, during, or after specific chapters of the novel).

You may therefore choose exactly the right exercise for the day, the objective, and the individual student or the specific group.

The Activity Sheets can be used for
- classroom or homework assignments.
- group discussion, individual study, or as work for partners or small groups.

You can use the Activity Sheets to concentrate on the particular needs of one or several students, while allowing others to work on their own or giving them experience in cooperative learning. Furthermore, each student may focus on the area in which he or she has difficulty, instead of having to perform routine exercises in topics already mastered.

Novel Ideas Classic is designed so you can select the materials that are right for your individual style of teaching and for the class's particular needs. You will naturally want to add to the resource books, drawing on your own insights and concerns. The main responsibility for introducing new skills will still rest with you, but the resource books will allow students to develop and reinforce their skills by practice that comes directly from their current reading assignments. With such support, you will find your task less arduous, and students will find their encounter with the literature more rewarding and more useful in developing their own skills and abilities.

Using Literature to Teach Skills

Rationale for Teaching *Lord of the Flies*

Few books have had as immediate and as widespread appeal among young people as *Lord of the Flies*. Those who began to teach it in the first years after its publication did so—as they had *Catcher in the Rye* and later would *The Lord of the Rings*—out of the most practical of motives: self-defense. Since students were reading it on their own, in preference to whatever traditional works had been assigned, the wisest course was to accept the inevitable and join forces with them. Although *Lord of the Flies* may no longer be the underground student favorite it was in the sixties, it still meets the most basic requirement of a good high school novel; the ability to hold a student's attention and interest.

Lord of the Flies tells a gripping story. It is fast moving, suspenseful, and capable of exciting a response on many levels, from the sheer excitement of the action to concern for the welfare of a favorite character to intense involvement in the moral issues the characters face. Moreover, the fact that it deals with a society made up solely of children makes it even more accessible to high school students than novels about war or other crises, which are typically set in the adult world.

A Springboard for Writing

The novel's dialogue, which may be troublesome to some students because of its use of British idiom, displays with great precision the rhythms and the peculiarities of spoken language—the different voices of older or younger boys, the coarse or the refined, the articulate or the tongue-tied. Golding's style invites close reading to challenge the most able student and shows the art of descriptive and narrative writing from which the whole class can benefit.

Teaching Strategies: Character

Golding depicts this conflict not as a battle among cardboard figures, but as a struggle among believable, realistic schoolboys. Ralph, Piggy, Simon, and Jack, in particular, stand out as individuals, deftly characterized by such physical touches as stature, hair color, and mannerisms, differentiated from one another even when they fight on the same side. Ralph's virtues, for example, which come closest to those of the stock schoolboy hero, are unlike those embodied in Piggy, the loyal and sensible counselor, or in Simon, the sensitive moral visionary.

Just as those good characters have flaws that weaken their power to confront the rising tide of barbarism on the island, Jack's climb to power and his growing influence over the other boys is made real by the strength of his ambition, the force of his personality, and his familiarity with command. Although Roger's followers are of necessity more like a uniform group than their opponents, his temperament differs from Jack's. The motives of a follower are shown as essentially different from those of a leader. Even the most minor characters, such as Percival Wemys Madison, are captured by the unerring eye for the substance and quirks of personality that typify Golding as both an experienced schoolteacher and a gifted writer. In its treatment of character, therefore, *Lord of the Flies* offers opportunities to discuss both literary technique and the complex blend of factors that exist in every individual.

Teaching Strategies: Scene and Event

Lord of the Flies is also a valuable teaching tool for its vivid depiction of scene and event. The descriptions of the island—its vegetation and surrounding waters—use precise images from nature to create a mood and set a tone for the events that follow. Action, whether small and ordinary, like lighting a fire, or abrupt and violent, like Piggy's death, is equally sharp and rich in detail.

Promotes Critical Thinking

Yet *Lord of the Flies* is far more than an adventure tale in a far-off place, a *Swiss Family Robinson* without the parents. Reading it calls on our familiarity with idealized stories about children who behave nobly under trial, and then goes on to question the validity of all of our stereotypes about "childhood innocence." Further, the novel explores the presence of evil in everyone, and the pernicious effects that anger, ambition, and fear have upon our efforts to live with one another. The issues Golding raises challenge our facile optimism and present a sobering, though not despairing picture of the human condition. The novel addresses the question of standing up for our beliefs, and at the same time avoiding self-deception about our actions or about how we would behave in adversity. Thematically, then, *Lord of the Flies* can open the doors to discussion of ethical problems, as well as of the "mingled yarn of good and ill" that most great writers tell us weaves the pattern of human life.

Synopsis of *Lord of the Flies*

Ralph, a fair-haired, athletic twelve-year-old, and Piggy, an overweight and spectacled youngster, meet on the beach of a Pacific island, where they have been marooned after their plane crashes, shot down during a war sometime in the future. Using a conch shell as a horn, Ralph assembles a crowd of boys and discovers that no adults have survived the crash.

The boys begin to set up an orderly society, in which a struggle for power develops between Ralph and Jack, the leader of a group of choirboys. Ralph wins out, and Jack and his followers offer themselves as a band of hunters. Jack and Ralph explore the island, accompanied by Simon, a smaller choirboy given to fainting, who later proves to have a mystical turn of mind. While exploring, Jack nearly kills a piglet but hesitates and the pig runs away; he vows that in the future he will not flinch at killing.

As Ralph and Simon organize the boys to build shelters and make a signal fire, Jack resists. He becomes obsessed with hunting and turns his followers into a war-painted band. So absorbed are the hunters in their fantasies of blood and conquest that they neglect the fire that might have signaled a passing ship about their plight. Ralph's unsuccessful efforts to reassert order result in a complete split between Jack's followers and his own.

As the dream of an idyllic, emancipated society fades, the younger children suffer nightmares, homesickness, and fear. When Samneric, a pair of twins, claim to have seen a real beast (in fact a dead paratrooper hanging by his harness), the boys begin to mistrust both their environment and one another. Three of the older boys—Jack, Roger, and Ralph—investigate this "beast" and erroneously confirm its existence. Jack, in a savage hunting excursion, kills a sow and leaves its head as a sacrificial offering to the "beast."

Simon decides to see the beast himself. On the way, he engages in a mystical confrontation with the sacrificial pig's head, the true "Lord of the Flies," which explains that the beast is the evil that dwells in each of them. With his newfound understanding of the beast's identity, Simon attempts to return to inform the others; he crawls however, into the tribal dance of Jack's savages and is speared to death.

Jack is now the chief of a mob, with Ralph, Piggy, and Samneric the only remnants of an orderly world. Jack, along with Roger, his lieutenant, invades Ralph's camp and steals Piggy's spectacles, their only instrument for lighting a fire. Piggy, virtually blinded, persuades Ralph to join him in an effort to retrieve them. Jack, however, who has by now tortured Samneric into joining his savages, attacks Ralph. Roger catapults a boulder that crushes Piggy and hurls his body into the sea.

Ralph flees for his life as Jack and his savages build a fire to burn away any cover he might find. Just as they discover him, the adult world, in the form of a British naval officer, arrives to rescue the boys. A cruiser has been attracted to the island by the fire and will return the boys, shorn of their innocence, to the outside world.

About the Author

William Golding

William Golding's career has been a remarkable mixture of the humdrum and the extraordinary. He spent many years of his life as a schoolteacher in a quiet English cathedral town. His naval experiences during World War II disrupted his peaceful world in a terrible way and contributed to his view of human nature as expressed in his first successful novel, *Lord of the Flies*.

Golding was born in 1911 in southwestern England. His father was a schoolmaster, and his mother, a dedicated feminist. He attended Oxford University, at first studying science but later switching to literature. In 1939, he began teaching at Bishop Wordsworth's School in Salisbury; the cathedral there provided the model for that in *The Spire*, his fifth novel.

When World War II began, Golding enlisted in the Royal Navy, serving as an officer on antiaircraft and antisubmarine vessels. After the war, he returned to teaching, but he was not the same man; the war had revealed to him the human potential for evil, a theme that he began to explore through writing. In 1954, he published *Lord of the Flies*; by 1961, he had completed four novels. After a year as writer-in-residence at Hollins College in Georgia, he retired from teaching to devote all his time to writing.

Although *Lord of the Flies* is Golding's best-known novel, all of his work show his literary skills and philosophical concerns. His fiction is remarkable for its range of settings and topics. He has written about Neanderthal man's conquest by *Homo sapiens* (*The Inheritors*, 1955), the arrogant ambition of a medieval cathedral builder (*The Spire*, 1964), and about the stifling narrowness of life in a modern English village (*The Pyramid*, 1967). Golding has even toyed with science fiction, a logical step for a writer whose books are often described as fables rather than novels. He turned his science fiction story, *Envoy Extraordinary*, into his only play, *The Brass Butterfly* (1958); it was later reissued with two other short novels in *The Scorpion God* (1971). In addition to fiction, he has also written a book of essays, *The Hot Gates* (1965).

Golding resembles Joseph Conrad, whose *Heart of Darkness* could be considered a companion piece to *Lord of the Flies*. Both authors deal with the dark side of human nature and use the sea as a theme. Golding's *Pincher Martin* (1956) also deals with a wartime castaway and *Free Fall* (1959) is set in a German prison camp. His *Darkness Visible* (1979) begins in the flames of a World War II air raid on London.

Whatever the setting, Golding's fiction is always concerned with the largest possible themes: the struggle between good and evil and the necessity of harnessing reason and emotion to prevent the selfishness and brutality that have marked human history—from the caveman and his club to the modern pilot and his bomber.

Socratic Discussion of *Lord of the Flies*

Lord of the Flies is a rich and relevant context in which students can think critically about an issue or a character's decision. Through Socratic discussion, an open forum for exploring ethics and issues, students are able to realize that different people find different answers to the same problem. Lead students as they read *Lord of the Flies* by stopping periodically for reflection and allowing time for discussion.

After Chapter 5

Ralph's meeting ends badly, when Jack disrupts the assembly and mocks Ralph's attempt to reinforce the rules. Jack leads a large group of boys away from the meeting, which ends in anarchy. Why is Ralph so obsessed with enforcing the rules? Why does society create rules? Would people be happier if they did whatever they desired? If one group of people becomes stronger and more powerful than the rest of society, does this give them the right to break the rules and take the law into their own hands?

If you had been one of the boys on the island, would you have joined the hunters or would you have supported Ralph? How do you think that people like Jack can gain so much power? Have you ever known anyone like Jack? Do people who are like Jack represent something you would like to be? Do others secretly admire rebels and rule-breakers because they are too afraid to break the rules themselves? Have you ever been persuaded to do something you knew was wrong to impress someone else?

After Chapter 11

Jack's tribe becomes evil and murderous gradually, in clearly defined stages. What is evil and where does it come from? Does evil exist outside a person, or is it a beast lurking within each of us? Is it a single person—such as Jack—who brings out the evil in others? Did power make Jack evil or did evil make him powerful? Is murder the ultimate display of power? Are the rules of civilization necessary to keep this evil in check?

When Piggy tries to reason with Jack's tribe, he is killed. In killing Simon and Piggy, the tribe has broken the greatest rule of all—the rule against murder. Would one member of the tribe have been able to kill Piggy without the others support? Does membership in a gang or any group give people power to do things they would be unable to do alone? What would make you hate someone enough to kill? Have you ever seen anyone persecuted because he or she was different in some way? Why do we hate people who seem to be different from us?

Writing Activities

Keep a Journal

Have students keep a "Journal of Fear," in which they respond to situations and quotations about fear as they appear in different parts of the novel. Students might also imagine they are with the boys on the island. Encourage them to record their feelings and to describe the threatening sights and sounds around them.

Write a Script or Dialogue

Have students write a script or dialogue (real or imagined) between major characters: for example, a conversation between two "littluns" on a wood-gathering expedition, or a confrontation between Ralph and Jack over a choice piece of fruit they find. Students might then perform a dramatic reading of their dialogues for the class.

Write a Story

Invite students to write a similar story using the first-person point of view. The story might take place on an island, a large ship, or in a submarine—any setting in which a group of children is isolated from the rest of society.

Write an Essay

Have students write an essay in response to questions based on the themes and/or characterization in the novel. For example:

1. How does the statement "The intellectual is often not fit to continue the evolutionary process in a society, and thus he is often sacrificed" apply to the society in Lord of the Flies and to our own society?
2. How does Jack's behavior reflect the statement "Evil survives in all societies"?
3. Of all the boys on the island, why does the author select only one—Ralph—to possess uncompromising ethics?

Write Descriptive Paragraphs

Ask students to write descriptive paragraphs, using scenes from the novel as models. Encourage students to pay special attention to creating mood.

Rewrite the Ending

Have students write a different ending to the story (beginning at Chapter 12).

Write a Play

Ask students to rewrite sections of the novel as a play and then stage their scenes.

Write a Newspaper Story

Invite students to write a newspaper story that reports the boys' rescue from the island.

Integrating Language Arts

Dramatize a Scene

Have students act out a scene from the novel, perhaps the initial struggle to start a fire, the killing of the first pig, the killing of Piggy, or Simon's confrontation with the "Lord of the Flies." SPEAKING/LISTENING

Extend the Story

Have students perform an improvised scene that might take place after the novel ends. Possible situations for the performance: SPEAKING/LISTENING

1. Samneric explaining the events on the island to their parents
2. a meeting between Jack's and Piggy's parents
3. a meeting between Ralph's and Simon's parents
4. Jack explaining in court the events of the final week on the island

Watch a Video

View one of the film versions of *Lord of the Flies*. Compare scenes, events, and characterizations with the novel. Afterward, ask students to share what they would include in their own film version of the novel. VIEWING/SPEAKING/LISTENING

Interview the Characters

Have each student choose a character to portray during an interview in which members of the class question that character's behavior and motives. Each student should justify his or her character's actions. SPEAKING/LISTENING

Relate the Story to Personal Experience

Discuss issues raised by *Lord of the Flies* that relate directly to students' lives. For example, ask students to consider and tell of their own experiences with gangs, cliques, clubs, or other groups. Was there an elected leader? Why or why not? Did peer pressure affect individual behavior or moral judgment? SPEAKING/LISTENING

Perform a Radio Play

Invite students to choose a sequence of scenes to dramatize and record. Collect musical instruments and other objects to make sound effects. Encourage students to think of songs and instrumental pieces that could be used as background music. If possible, have the recording broadcast over your school's public address system. WRITING/SPEAKING/LISTENING

Integrating the Curriculum

Social Studies
Have students investigate events that reflect extreme evil: the Nazi concentration camps; the systematic destruction of Native Americans; the Manson murders; gangland slayings; and so forth. Students' results can be presented orally or in writing.

Art
Allow students to choose one of the following art projects: **1.** Sketch the painted faces of some of the hunters. **2.** Draw a picture of the "Lord of the Flies." **3.** Make a model of the island.

Music
Ask students to collect a variety of music, classical and contemporary, to accompany different events in the novel—music for sunrises, for gathering fruit, for hunting pigs, or for building fires.

Drama
Lead students in improvising and acting out a science fiction version of *Lord of the Flies*, in which schoolchildren have crash-landed on a strange but inhabitable planet.

More Books to Read
- *Butterfly Revolution* by William Butler. In many ways, this novel is a contemporary (though less sophisticated version) of *Lord of the Flies*, set at a summer camp. Students might explore similarities and differences in the two novels. This novel could serve as a substitute reading assignment to *Lord of the Flies* for students who may have difficulty with the sophistication of Golding's novel.
- *Deathwatch* by Robb White. An examination of the inescapable evil of man, this suspense thriller deals with an unscrupulous, conniving businessman's cruelty toward an honest, innocent college student.
- *Heart of Darkness* by Joseph Conrad. Ask students to look in this novel for a definition of the "Heart of Darkness." Have them keep in mind the reference in *Lord of the Flies* to Ralph's sobbing for the "darkness of man's heart," and the conversation between Simon and the "Lord of the Flies." Ask students to note similarities in theme as well as in style, mood, and tone in Golding's and Conrad's writing.
- *The Inheritors* by William Golding. This novel depicts the struggle for survival by the remaining few Neanderthals as they are forced out by the first *Homo sapiens*. Students can examine variations on the theme.
- *Pincher Martin* by William Golding. This novel further explores the theme of evil. It deals with the ability of a shipwrecked sailor to survive both physically and mentally. The sailor is a tragic character who is unaware of the evil inside him and thus is unable to control his violent feelings or behavior. Students might compare him with Jack.

Teaching Strategies

Activity 1
Word Meaning: Leadership

Critical-Creative Thinking. This prereading activity is designed for students at all ability levels. Its purpose is to acquaint the student with an essential theme in the novel: leadership. Students should complete this exercise individually, and then share their responses with the class.

From their exposure to U.S. history courses, World War II films and discussions, and public examinations of the Holocaust, students should be able to draw on material to discuss the leadership characteristics of Adolf Hitler. First, draw attention to the characteristics that made Hitler succeed as a dictator (Jack's similarity to Hitler can be explored during the reading of the novel). Students might then list and discuss characteristics of other people, past and present, whom they consider successful leaders. Alternatively, students might rank order characteristics of each boy on the island. This activity will require careful examination of the pros and cons of the possible leaders. Emphasize that leadership is an important theme in the novel, and that the quality of leadership is only as good as the ethics of the leader. The last question on Activity Sheet 1 may be used either for discussion or as a writing assignment.

Review this activity before students complete the decision-making activity (Activity Sheet 3) that involves selecting a leader from the boys on the island.

Activity 2
Reading Guide: Chapters 1–3

Reading Comprehension/Critical-Creative Thinking. These questions can guide students' reading of the novel and help them to focus their attention on the book's major points. These questions can also serve as a "road map" for less able readers and as a source of questions for periodic quizzes. Review the Guide with students before they read the novel. Most of the questions require literal understanding. Questions 11 and 12 require inferential or critical thinking to answer.

You may suggest that students jot down brief answers to the questions on the pages themselves, or you can ask students to keep a journal or a notebook in which to record more detailed responses as they read.

Activity 3
Characterization

Critical Thinking. You may wish to review Activity 1 with the class before they begin this activity, which can be worked on individually or in small groups. After students have voted, invite them to debate their choice of candidate. Voting could be extended into a dramatic exercise, in which students take the part of each of the characters and give speeches to explain why they should be elected.

Activity 4
Cause and Effect (Literal)

Reading Comprehension. This is a literal-level exercise designed specifically to help less able readers develop the ability to determine cause and effect relationships. You may assign it after students have finished reading Chapter 3, as either an in-class or homework assignment. Before assigning this exercise, however, you should discuss the relationship between cause and effect with the class. For each item, discuss the relationship between the cause and its effect(s). After students complete the exercise independently, they should explain the direct cause and effect link for each item. You might use students' responses for diagnostic purposes, reviewing completed activity sheets to determine which students appear to be having trouble understanding the novel to this point. Ask students to pay close attention to events in the novel and to consider how each action may affect subsequent events.

Activity 5
Characterization (Literal/Inferential)

Literary Analysis. This activity helps students to focus on various aspects of the development of characterization. It can be assigned at any point during the reading of the opening chapters in the novel. You might save this exercise until everyone has read through the third chapter, or ask students to keep the activity sheet in their notebooks and fill in parts of it as they read the novel. In conjunction with this exercise, you should review with the class the various techniques an author uses to develop character. After doing this activity, students will have a deeper understanding of the characters and will be able to visualize them more clearly. The last question provides background for a lively discussion on friendship. You might point out how the friendship between Simon, Jack, and Ralph deteriorates after their initial exploration of the island, leaving Ralph particularly confused about Jack's behavior.

Activity 6
Cause and Effect (Critical)

Reading Comprehension. This activity, to be completed after Chapter 3, enables students to use their personal ingenuity along with their skills in understanding cause and effect relationships. They can set goals for survival and rescue individually or in groups. After, they can debate their choices as a class. Students at all ability levels can do this activity. After completing the exercise independently, students should explain the direct cause and effect link for each item. You might use students' responses for diagnostic purposes, reviewing completed activity sheets to determine which students appear to be having trouble understanding the novel to this point.

Activity 7
Reading Guide: Chapters 4–6

Reading Comprehension/Critical-Creative Thinking. These questions guide students' reading of the novel and help to focus students' attention on the major points of the book. Questions 6 and 7 can be used to stimulate a lively discussion. Questions 6, 7, and 8 require critical or inferential thinking to answer.

Activity 8
Point of View

Literary Analysis. The assignment will require much prewriting time and discussion. Make sure that all students have read the relevant passages in the novel before you begin the discussion on what each character saw and thought about the action. Tell students that *point of view* means the way a person perceives events. Ask students to imagine they are present, seeing events from each character's point of view. When students have finished the assignment, they might share their writing in groups. To extend this activity, students may also write "point-of-view" essays about an issue in their school or community.

Activity 9
Mood

Written Language. The purpose here is to focus on a specific composition skill: writing to create a mood. Since the novel reflects many moods, you might wish to make this particular skill part of a series of related composition assignments. The final paragraph may be composed on the back of the page or on a separate sheet of paper; it provides a chance for students to exercise their skill in creative writing.

Activity 10
Characterization (Inferential)

Literary Analysis. After the class has read through Chapter 5, assign this activity sheet. This is a good activity for group work because students can share the task of searching through the novel for quotations that reveal character traits. You might also divide the class into groups, with each group searching for quotations from each character. You might choose to use the last activity to encourage a discussion of character and self-knowledge.

Activity 11
Words in Context

Vocabulary. This activity introduces eight words that are used to describe the main characters in the novel. A definition and a synonym for each word is given. Students are asked to complete a fill-in-the-blank exercise. Then they can check their answers against the original sentences in the book; chapter locations are provided at the end of each sentence in the exercise. You might take this opportunity to teach students how to skim quickly for important information. The second part of the activity requires students to use the underlined word in an original sentence.

Activity 12
Critical Reading

Reading Comprehension. (Because of the relative difficulty of this exercise, you may wish to restrict all or parts of this exercise to the more advanced students in the class.) After students have read through Chapter 6, ask them to find specific passages in the novel to support their answers to the first part of the exercise. Students might debate key issues related to the two types of societies reflected in the novel before writing the essays in the second and third exercises. These questions also provide an opportunity to discuss symbolism in the novel and what each character might represent. After the activity, you might divide the class into two groups—one supporting Jack and the other, Ralph—to continue the debate.

Activity 13
Reading Guide: Chapters 7–9

Reading Comprehension/Critical-Creative Thinking. Students may need to review the incident referred to in question 7. After they have answered this question, you might conduct a discussion of the event, drawing parallels to other male initiation rites in our society, such as hazing, and the importance of these rituals in sports and in the military.

Activity 14
Cause and Effect (Inferential)

Reading Comprehension/Inferential Thinking. This activity combines students' understanding of character with their skill in recognizing cause and effect relationships. After they complete the exercise independently or in small groups, have students explain to the class the direct cause and effect link in each item. You might use students' responses for diagnostic purposes, reviewing completed activity sheets to determine which students appear to be having trouble understanding the novel to this point.

Activity 15
Sequence of Events (Literal)

Reading Comprehension. This activity contains a general practice exercise to help less able students recognize sequence of events. Before assigning this activity, point out the usefulness of signal words to indicate sequence of events. The class might look for specific examples of signal words at different places in the novel and/or in other printed materials. After students complete the activity sheet, they can meet in small groups to compare their versions of the final paragraph, giving reasons for their choices in ordering the sentences. You might extend this activity by encouraging students to use the listed words in short narratives of their own.

Activity 16
Theme (Literal)

Literary Analysis. Taking students step by step through the parts of the novel that they have read so far, this activity helps students review incidents that illustrate various types of fear. The last question provides an excellent opportunity for students to put together some of the insights they have gained about this theme. Although the exercise is a relatively easy task (involving locating answers in the text), it can be valuable for students at all ability levels. You might also use this opportunity to teach students how to skim a text quickly for information.

Activity 17
Critical Reading

Reading Comprehension. This activity is a critical-creative reading comprehension activity in which students are asked to explain and interpret Simon's mystical experience on the mountain. Tell students that there is no right or wrong answer, but that they should be ready to justify their interpretations. A prewriting discussion might help students tackle this activity. You might want to point out that epilepsy was considered a "divine" affliction in ancient times, and thus is entirely in keeping with Simon's spiritual identity. Students might also look through the novel to find other references to Simon's visionary power.

Activity 18
Reading Guide: Chapters 10–12

Reading Comprehension/Critical-Creative Thinking. These questions can serve as a "road map" for less able readers and as a source of questions for periodic quizzes. Most of the questions require literal understanding. Questions 7, 10, and 11 require inferential or critical thinking to answer.

You may suggest that students jot down brief answers to the questions on the pages themselves, or you can ask students to keep a journal or a notebook in which to record more detailed responses as they read.

Activity 19
Antonyms

Vocabulary. The vocabulary from the novel is extensive and difficult. Be sure to devote enough time to clarifying word meanings and their usage before assigning these worksheets. The activities—such as this one focusing on synonyms and antonyms—are suitable for both individual and small group study.

The activity lists ten vocabulary words that reflect the theme of evil throughout the book. For each word, a definition and a synonym are given. Begin by pronouncing and discussing with students these words, their possible definitions, and their synonyms. You might ask students to write the definitions in their own words or to write additional synonyms for these words on a separate sheet of paper. Students are asked to write on the worksheet an antonym for each underlined word. Small group work is recommended for this activity. Bring the groups together to discuss acceptable antonyms. As a follow-up activity, you might wish to encourage students to write short descriptive passages, using as many words from this page as possible.

Activity 20
Structural Analysis

Vocabulary. The first activity involves constructing noun and adjective forms of verbs. All of the words appeared previously on Activity Sheet 19. Before beginning this activity, you might ask students to pronounce each word and suggest a meaning for it.

The second activity involves writing a sentence for the noun form and the adjective form of each verb. You might use this activity to encourage investigation of other related word groups.

Activity 21
Theme

Literary Analysis. In this exercise, students are called on to write extensively about the causes and effects of fear on each of the main characters in the novel. They then write a culminating essay on the overall theme. After students finish writing, discuss their answers. You might also ask them to compare the effects of fear on each of the characters.

Activity 22
Word Meaning

Vocabulary. This activity is a crossword puzzle that utilizes all vocabulary words in the unit. The clues are nearly verbatim definitions of the words used in the other vocabulary activity sheets. Although this puzzle could be used as a quiz after all the words have been studied, it might be more appropriately used as a game

Lord of the Flies

to reinforce the word meanings at the end of the unit. If the puzzle seems too difficult, you might provide a list of some of the words on the chalkboard. Students could also use these words to create their own crossword puzzles, using the same words from *Lord of the Flies*. Students could then exchange their crossword puzzles with a partner.

Activity 23
Sequence

Reading Comprehension. This exercise requires students to recall the sequence of events in selected sections of *Lord of the Flies* after they have finished reading the novel. Ask students to do their sequencing from memory, or direct them to use their books to check as they go along. After this exercise, you can review the students' responses and discuss why the sequence of events is important in developing the plot, characterization, and themes of the novel. You may use this sheet to diagram the sequence of events on the chalkboard.

Activity 24
Theme

Literary Analysis. This activity brings the class's attention to related themes in the novel. It is a good review exercise for the entire novel. Some of the statements in this exercise reflect more than one theme, and this variation may provide opportunities to discuss other themes in the novel. The second part of the activity sheet allows students to consider how different symbols in the novel illustrate one or more of the themes. You might alter the directions for this second section by assigning a different symbol to each of several small groups of students so that when the entire class discusses the symbols, all major symbols will have been covered.

Activity 25
Characterization (Inferential/Critical)

Literary Analysis. This is a more challenging activity that requires students to draw inferences from their reading about characters and to think critically about the interactions of characters and events throughout the novel. This activity sheet should provide background ideas for lively class discussions about the qualities of the main characters. (The final activity on this worksheet can provide an interesting opportunity for dramatic improvisation by pairs of students.)

Activity 26
Characterization (Inferential/Critical)

Literary Analysis. This final literary analysis activity is a high-level exercise that requires students to bring together their understanding of character, theme, and cause and effect relationships from this unit. The students' short paragraphs can be used as a basis for class discussions, or a class discussion can be used as background for helping students write responses on this activity sheet. Before assigning this activity sheet, you might discuss what evolution is and how it is based on adaptability to the environment. You might also wish to discuss the theme of "survival of the fittest." Students familiar with the theory might report briefly on the topic. These exercises can be adapted for less able students.

Tests 1–5

Although you may prefer to use your own unit evaluation, these tests are offered as models that contain a variety of the types of items that might be used to measure students' recall and understanding of the novel *Lord of the Flies*. These tests include a measure of vocabulary knowledge, a section on character identification, a series of objective items related to facts and ideas in the novel, and essay questions. You may use part or all of this test section, as appropriate, with different groups of students.

Additional Teaching Strategy Suggestions

Vocabulary Development

Keep a Vocabulary Notebook
Lord of the Flies is full of rich language and vivid descriptions. Ask students to keep a vocabulary notebook of the descriptive words they come across as they read the novel. These words can be categorized as words used to describe the characters or the environment (the mirages of the friendly side of the island; the lush jungle of the interior; or the harsh seascapes of the unfriendly, rocky side). Later, after they have written a sufficient number of words, students can write descriptive passages using the words.

List Words in Categories
The idea of listing new words according to categories can be extended to include all words that convey the dark forces that threaten the boys and their society (for example, *malevolent, oppressive, demoniac, menacing*) or words in any other category that students suggest.

Focus on Semantics
Semantics—the positive and negative connotations of words—can also be a focus for word study. It is a particularly relevant study for a novel in which things so often are not what they seem. Students can compile lists of new words; after giving the denotation (the literal meaning of the word), students can tell whether each word has positive or negative associations and why.

Reading Comprehension

Sequence Events
Students can keep an ongoing record (individual or class) through a Time Line or a Flow Chart of major events in the novel. A master chart could be drawn up to assign different chapters to small groups of students.

Draw Conclusions
Students can discuss "If . . . then . . ." situations in the novel. (Examples: If the boys had kept the fire going at the top of the mountain, then what might have happened as the first ship passed? If Jack had been elected leader at the beginning, then what might have happened?)

ACTIVITY 1

Word Meaning: Leadership

1. Below is a list of leadership characteristics. Examine the list, then add two other characteristics you think are important in a leader on the blanks provided.

   ____ intelligence   ____ common sense

   ____ ethics   ____ courage

   ____ physical strength   ____ power

   ____ military prowess   ____ _____

   ____ ambition   ____ _____

   Now rank the characteristics above in order of importance. Write a *1* in the blank next to the characteristic you consider the most important for a leader. Write a *2* by the next most important, a *3* by the most important after that, and so forth.

2. Rank order these same characteristics in Adolf Hitler. Then do the same for two other leaders whom you know about. Write each leader's name in the blank provided.

Adolf Hitler	**Leader #2** _____	**Leader #3** _____
____ intelligence	____	____
____ ethics	____	____
____ physical strength	____	____
____ military prowess	____	____
____ ambition	____	____
____ common sense	____	____
____ courage	____	____
____ power	____	____

3. Which leader's ranking most closely matches the ideal you formed in question 1? Explain your answer, and then tell why you believe that leader possesses the kind of characteristics you think are most important. Use a separate sheet of paper for your response.

Lord of the Flies
Novel Ideas Classic © 1997, Sundance

Critical-Creative Thinking
Prereading • LEVEL 2

Name: _____

ACTIVITY 2

Reading Guide: Chapters 1–3

Use these questions to guide your reading and understanding of the novel. Preview the questions before you begin the chapters. Write your responses in the space after each question, or write more complete responses in a journal.

1. What is the setting of the story?

2. What events led to the boys' arrival on the island?

3. Why couldn't Jack kill the pig?

4. Who emerged as leader of the group? Why?

5. What power did the conch give the person who holds it?

6. How did the snake-thing make the boys feel?

7. What did the group decide to do to be rescued?

8. How was Piggy indirectly helpful in starting the fire?

9. What important task did Piggy forget to do for Ralph?

10. Which do you think was more important to the boys' survival: hunting for meat or building shelters? Why?

11. Why was it so difficult for Ralph and Jack to communicate with each other?

Lord of the Flies
Novel Ideas Classic © 1997, Sundance

Reading Comprehension/Critical-Creative Thinking
Prereading • LEVEL 2

Name: _____

ACTIVITY 3

Characterization

Imagine that you are with the boys on the island. For whom would you vote to be the leader? List pros and cons for each of the candidates below. Then tell why you would or would not vote for that person. (Keep in mind the qualities you listed on Activity Sheet 1.)

Cast Your Ballot

Ralph

Pros: _____

Cons: _____

Reasons: _____

_____

Jack

Pros: _____

Cons: _____

Reasons: _____

_____

Piggy

Pros: _____

Cons: _____

Reasons: _____

_____

Write-in Candidate

Pros: _____

Cons: _____

Reasons: _____

_____

Lord of the Flies
Novel Ideas Classic © 1997, Sundance

Critical Thinking
After Chapter 3 • LEVEL 2

Name: _____

ACTIVITY 4

Cause and Effect

Give the cause of each event or situation by writing the letter of the phrase that best completes each sentence.

_____ 1. Piggy's glasses were valuable to the boys because
   a. the boys used them to search for food.   b. the boys used them to light the fire.
   c. the boys used them to drink water.

_____ 2. The boys lit a fire on top of the mountain because they
   a. hoped a passing ship would see the smoke.   b. needed the fire to keep warm.
   c. needed the fire to cook meat.

_____ 3. The boys arrived on the island because of
   a. a camping trip.   b. a shipwreck.   c. a plane crash.

_____ 4. The boys came to the assemblies because
   a. Ralph blew the conch.   b. meat would be cooked and served.
   c. afterward, they could go swimming.

_____ 5. In the assemblies, the boy holding the conch
   a. is the chief.   b. has the right to speak.   c. must gather fruit for the others.

_____ 6. At first, the boys were happy on the island because
   a. they thought they would be rescued quickly.
   b. there was lots of food and drink.
   c. they thought of it as an adventure.

_____ 7. Ralph became angry with the group because
   a. they wouldn't go hunting.   b. they wouldn't build shelters.
   c. they wouldn't come to the assemblies.

_____ 8. At the first assembly, Jack thought that he should be the leader because
   a. he was "head boy" in the choir.   b. he had won the vote.
   c. he wanted Piggy to like him.

_____ 9. The boys had trouble exploring the jungle because
   a. pigs kept charging at them.   b. there were too many rocks.
   c. the roots and stems of the creepers were thick and tangled.

_____ 10. The boys started a huge forest fire
   a. because they wanted more burned wood.   b. because they wanted to dance.
   c. by accident.

Lord of the Flies
Novel Ideas Classic © 1997, Sundance

Reading Comprehension
After Chapter 3 • LEVEL 1

Name: _____

ACTIVITY 5

Characterization

In a novel, we learn about characters from the author's descriptions of them, from how they act and what they say, and from what others say about them. As you read through the first chapters of *Lord of the Flies*, jot down what you learn about each of the main characters.

Piggy

1. In Chapter 1, what words and phrases are used to describe Piggy

    physically: _____

    intellectually: _____

    socially: _____

2. How do others respond to Piggy? _____

    _____

Ralph

1. From what you learn in the opening chapters, describe Ralph

    physically: _____

    intellectually: _____

    socially: _____

2. How do others respond to Ralph? _____

    _____

Jack

1. Read Chapter 1. Describe Jack's appearance: _____

    _____

2. At the first meeting, Jack arrogantly says, "I ought to be the chief." What does that statement tell you about Jack? _____

    _____

3. How do others feel about Jack at this point? _____

    _____

If you were on the island, which one of those three boys would you try to become friends with and why? Write your answer on the back of this page or on a separate sheet of paper.

Lord of the Flies
Novel Ideas Classic © 1997, Sundance

Literary Analysis
During Chapters 1–3 • LEVEL 2

ACTIVITY 6

Cause and Effect

Imagine you are one of the boys on the island. You know what resources are available to you and to everyone else. No leader has been chosen. Survival has been left up to the individual. You are on your own! Develop your strategy for survival and rescue.

Goals: State three goals, in order of importance.

1. _____
2. _____
3. _____

Explain the reasons for the order you chose:

_____
_____
_____
_____
_____
_____

Now write a plan for achieving each goal. You must use only the resources available on the island in the novel. If other people are needed in order to accomplish your goal(s), indicate how you will obtain their help.

Goal 1:

What do you need? _____

How will you get it? _____
_____

Goal 2:

What do you need? _____

How will you get it? _____
_____

Goal 3:

What do you need? _____

How will you get it? _____
_____

Lord of the Flies
Novel Ideas Classic © 1997, Sundance

Reading Comprehension
After Chapter 3 • LEVEL 2

ACTIVITY 7

Reading Guide: Chapters 4–6

Use these questions to guide your reading and understanding of the novel. Preview the questions before you begin the chapters. Write your responses in the space after each question, or write more complete responses in a journal.

1. What is the purpose of dazzle paint?

2. Why does the ship fail to see the boys?

3. Why does Jack allow the fire to go out?

4. Why does Percival Wemys Madison cry all the time?

5. What is the beast that Samneric sees?

6. Why do the boys clamor "Kill the pig. Cut her throat. Bash her in!"?

7. Is there actually a beast? How do you know?

8. Does Jack really want to be rescued? Why?

Lord of the Flies
Novel Ideas Classic © 1997, Sundance

Reading Comprehension/Critical-Creative Thinking
After Chapter 3 • LEVEL 2

Point of View

Different people can experience the same event in different ways. What you think about an event is determined by your personality and by your feelings about the other people involved. The way people see an event and what they think about it is called **point of view.**

Imagine that you are each of the characters listed below. Below the character's name, write a brief paragraph describing how he felt about the fire going out and the subsequent argument. Be sure to write about the event from that character's point of view.

Jack

Ralph

Piggy

Roger

Lord of the Flies

Literary Analysis
After Chapter 4 • LEVEL 3

Name: _____

ACTIVITY 9

Mood

A **mood** is a state of feeling. An author uses specific words and phrases to create a particular mood. Read the passage below from *Lord of the Flies*. Study the passage carefully and, in the space labeled "mood," write a word or a phrase that describes the mood or impression that passage creates.

> The first rhythm that they became used to was the slow swing from dawn to quick dusk. They accepted the pleasures of morning, the bright sun, the whelming sea and sweet air, as a time when play was good and life so full that hope was not necessary and therefore forgotten. Toward noon, as the floods of light fell more nearly to the perpendicular, the stark colors of the morning were smoothed in pearl and opalescence; and the heat . . . became a blow that they ducked, running to the shade and lying there, perhaps sleeping. (Chapter 4)

Mood: _____

Words that created the mood:

_____ _____ _____ _____

_____ _____ _____ _____

Now, write a paragraph to create your own specific mood. You may wish to create a mood or impression that is exciting and suspenseful, one that is angry and violent, or perhaps one that is quiet and peaceful.

1. What is the mood or impression you want to create?

   _____
   _____
   _____
   _____

2. Write words and phrases here that might help you create that mood or impression:

   _____
   _____
   _____
   _____

3. Now write a paragraph using those words and phrases to create the particular mood or impression. Use the back of this page or write your response on a separate sheet of paper.

Lord of the Flies
Novel Ideas Classic © 1997, Sundance

Written Language
After Chapter 5 • LEVEL 2

ACTIVITY 10

Characterization

What characters say and think reveals what kind of people they are. On a separate sheet of paper, explain what the quotations below show about each character.

Piggy

1. In Chapter 5, Piggy says, "Life . . . is scientific, that's what it is."
   What does that statement tell you about Piggy?

2. Write one other statement from the novel that supports Piggy's view of life. Be sure to include the page reference.

Ralph

1. Ralph says in Chapter 5, "We've got to talk about this fear and decide there's nothing in it. I'm frightened myself, sometimes; only that's nonsense! Like bogies. Then, when we've decided, we can start again and be careful about things like the fire."
   What does that tell you about Ralph's character?

2. Write one other statement from the novel that shows this characteristic of Ralph's. Be sure to include the page reference.

Jack

1. What is the most important goal in Jack's life?

2. What does that tell you about his character?

3. Jack says, "If you're hunting sometimes you catch yourself feeling as if — . . . There's nothing in it of course. Just a feeling. But you can feel as if you're not hunting, but— being hunted, as if something's behind you all the time in the jungle." What does that tell you about Jack's character?

At this point in the novel, which of the characters do you think understands himself best? Justify your choice. Write your answer on the back of this page or on a separate sheet of paper.

Lord of the Flies
Novel Ideas Classic © 1997, Sundance

Literary Analysis
After Chapter 5 • LEVEL 2

ACTIVITY 11

Words in Context

The following words are used to describe main characters in the novel. A definition and a synonym are given for each word.

Word	Definition	Synonym
awesome	inspiring a mixed feeling of fear and wonder	dreadful
diffident	lacking confidence in oneself	shy
embroiled	contused or mixed up	entangled
sinewy	lean and muscular	strong
inarticulate	unable to speak clearly	not expressive
incomprehension	failure to understand	confusion
ludicrous	causing laughter because of absurdity	ridiculous
charitable	giving money or other help to the needy	generous

Using the words from the list above, fill in the blanks in the sentences below.

1. He turned a half-concealed face up to Roger and answered the _____ of his gaze. (Chapter 4)

2. Simon became _____ in his effort to express mankind's essential illness. (Chapter 5)

3. But Piggy, for all his _____ body, had brains. (Chapter 5)

4. Piggy, finding himself uncomfortably _____ , slid the conch to Ralph's knees and sat down. (Chapter 6)

5. He sought, _____ in his happiness, to include them in the thing that had happened. (Chapter 4)

6. Beside the pool his _____ body held up a mask that drew their eyes and appalled them. (Chapter 4)

7. He looked in astonishment, no longer at himself but at an _____ stranger. (Chapter 4)

8. _____ , Simon allowed his pace to slacken until he was walking side by side with Ralph and looking up at him through the coarse black hair that now fell to his eyes. (Chapter 6)

When you have finished, check your answers by referring to the sentence in the novel. Then, on the back of this page, write a sentence of your own, using the word correctly.

Lord of the Flies
Novel Ideas Classic © 1997, Sundance

Vocabulary
After Chapter 6 • LEVEL 2

Name: _____

ACTIVITY 12

Critical Reading

Ralph and Jack are both leaders, but they have different qualities. Each tries to create a society that promotes his own qualities. Write down the qualities of each boy and those of the societies they try to create.

Ralph

Personal qualities: _____
_____
_____
_____

Qualities of his society: _____
_____
_____
_____

Jack

Personal qualities: _____
_____
_____
_____

Qualities of his society: _____
_____
_____
_____

From what you have read so far, write a short paragraph to explain which type of society you expect will dominate by the end of the novel and why you think it will—or should—dominate. Use the back of this page or write your answer on a separate sheet of paper.

In a short paragraph, tell which aspects of Ralph's society you see reflected in our society, and in what ways Jack's thinking is reflected. Use the back of this page or write your answer on a separate sheet of paper.

Lord of the Flies
Novel Ideas Classic © 1997, Sundance

Reading Comprehension
After Chapter 6 • LEVEL 3

Name: _____

ACTIVITY 13

Reading Guide: Chapters 7–9

Use these questions to guide your reading and understanding of the novel. Preview the questions before you begin the chapters. Write your responses in the space after each question, or write more complete responses in a journal.

1. Why did Ralph daydream about home?

2. What game did the boys play after spearing the wild boar?

3. Did all the boys believe they had seen a beast near the pink granite?

4. Why did Jack form his own group?

5. What did Jack call his group? How is that a fitting name?

6. How did the boys kill the sow?

7. How is the sow-killing incident like an initiation?

8. Why was the stick sharpened at both ends?

9. What was the "Lord of the Flies"?

10. Was the "Lord of the Flies" really speaking to Simon? How do you know?

11. Was Simon actually "batty"? What evidence do you have?

12. What did Simon discover about the beast?

13. What was Simon trying to do when the boys kill him?

14. Why did the boys kill Simon?

15. When the boys killed Simon, did they know what they were doing?

Lord of the Flies
Novel Ideas Classic © 1997, Sundance

Reading Comprehension/Critical-Creative Thinking
After Chapter 6 • LEVEL 2

Name: _____

ACTIVITY 14

Cause and Effect

Below are several statements that describe one character's feelings about another character. For each, list the causes, or reasons, for that feeling and then list the effects, or results of that feeling.

1. Jack hates Piggy.

   Causes: _____
   _____

   Effects: _____
   _____
   _____

2. Piggy is afraid of Jack.

   Causes: _____
   _____

   Effects: _____
   _____
   _____

3. Ralph thinks Simon is batty.

   Causes: _____
   _____

   Effects: _____
   _____
   _____

4. Jack hates Ralph.

   Causes: _____
   _____

   Effects: _____
   _____
   _____

Lord of the Flies
Novel Ideas Classic © 1997, Sundance

Reading Comprehension/Inferential Thinking
After Chapter 9 • LEVEL 2

ACTIVITY 15

Sequence of Events

Often a written passage will have "signal" words and expressions—such as *first, then, afterward, finally,* or *next*—to indicate the sequence, or order, of events.

Read the following sentences. Circle any words or expressions that signal the sequence of events.

> From the woods came a quick patter of hoofs.
>
> Jack and the other hunters followed.
>
> The spear hit the pig between the shoulders.
>
> First, Jack bent over, looking for the pig's trail.
>
> After being hit, the pig squealed and crashed into the forest.
>
> He found clues: a cracked twig and the impression of a hoof.
>
> The hunters found the pig tangled in the creepers.
>
> Jack raised his right arm and hurled the spear with all his strength.
>
> The hunters surrounded the pig and stuck it with spears.
>
> Finally, the pig died.

Now, arrange the above sentences in the correct sequence and write them in paragraph form in the space provided or on a separate sheet of paper.

_____
_____
_____
_____
_____
_____
_____
_____
_____
_____
_____
_____

Lord of the Flies
Novel Ideas Classic © 1997, Sundance

Reading Comprehension
After Chapter 9 • LEVEL 1

Name: _____

ACTIVITY 16

Theme

Throughout *Lord of the Flies*, the author describes fear in many different ways. Read about the events referred to in the following phrases. Then describe what the characters experience, and how they deal with those fears.

1. Describe the little boy's fear. (Chapter 2) _____
_____

2. Describe the fear the littluns have. (Chapter 3) _____
_____

3. Why are the littluns frightened? (Chapter 3) _____
_____

4. How do the older boys decide to deal with fear? (Chapter 5) _____
_____

5. According to Piggy, how do grownups deal with fear? (Chapter 5) _____
_____

6. What are the twins afraid of? (Chapter 6) _____
_____

7. What is Ralph afraid of? (Chapter 7) _____
_____

8. How does Jack try to satisfy the beast, and why does he do that? (Chapter 8) _____
_____

9. What type of fear does the sow experience? (Chapter 8) _____
_____

10. Why is Simon afraid? How does he deal with his fear? (Chapter 8) _____
_____

11. Select a character from the novel and answer the following questions using the back of this page or a separate sheet of paper.

    a. What is that character afraid of?   b. How does he deal with those fears?

    c. Do you think he handles his fears well? Explain.

Lord of the Flies
Novel Ideas Classic © 1997, Sundance

Literary Analysis
After Chapter 9 • LEVEL 1

ACTIVITY 17

Critical Reading

Simon is the visionary of *Lord of the Flies*, a prophet sacrificed by his more savage companions. After his mystical experience with the sacrificial head, Simon climbs down from the mountain to bring his new knowledge to the other boys. Imagine you are Simon. Write an explanation of what you experienced on the mountain, followed by an interpretation of what you heard.

Lord of the Flies
Novel Ideas Classic © 1997, Sundance

Reading Comprehension
After Chapter 9 • LEVEL 3

Name: _____

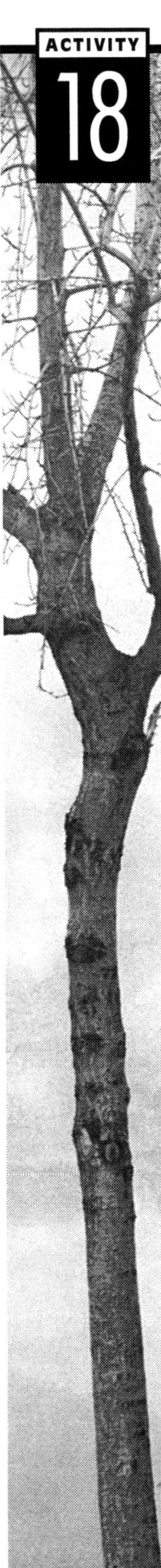

ACTIVITY 18

Reading Guide: Chapters 10–12

Use these questions to guide your reading and understanding of the novel. Preview the questions before you begin the chapters. Write your responses in the space after each question, or write more complete responses in a journal.

1. Who is left in Ralph's group?

2. What does Jack build to keep away trespassers?

3. Why do Jack and Roger invade Ralph's camp at night?

4. What do Ralph and Piggy decide to do after they are attacked?

5. What happens to Piggy?

6. Why is the stick in Chapter 12 sharpened at both ends?

7. Now that Ralph is alone, what do you think he should do?

8. Does Ralph now believe that Jack will kill him?

9. At the end of the story, how do the rescuers know someone is on the island?

10. Do you think the naval officer believes that two boys were killed?

11. Why does Ralph cry?

Lord of the Flies
Novel Ideas Classic © 1997, Sundance

Reading Comprehension/Critical-Creative Thinking
After Chapter 9 • LEVEL 2

ACTIVITY 19

Antonyms

One of the major themes of *Lord of the Flies* is evil. In the novel, evil involves fear, hatred, and ugliness. The underlined words below reflect this theme. Each is followed by a definition, a synonym, and the chapter number in which the word appears. Read the definition and the synonym, then find each underlined word in the appropriate chapter of the book. Read the sentence containing the word. Then, write an *antonym* (word with an opposite meaning) for each underlined word in the space provided.

1. intimidated: to be made timid or afraid; threatened (Chapter 1)

   _____

2. oppressive: hard to put up with; overbearing (Chapter 3)

   _____

3. malevolently: wishing evil or harm to others; with spite (Chapter 4)

   _____

4. derisive: showing contempt or scorn; ridiculing (Chapter 5)

   _____

5. condemnation: an infliction of penalty; conviction (Chapter 5)

   _____

6. daunting: making afraid; discouraging (Chapter 7)

   _____

7. contemptuously: showing an attitude of worthlessness; scornfully (Chapter 8)

   _____

8. furtive: sly; sneaky (Chapter 8)

   _____

9. obscene: indecent; repulsive (Chapter 8)

   _____

10. abominable: disgusting; vile; loathsome (Chapter 9)

    _____

Lord of the Flies
Novel Ideas Classic © 1997, Sundance

Vocabulary
After Chapter 11 • LEVEL 2

Structural Analysis

Form a noun by adding **-ion** or **-ation** to a verb. In this way, for example, *exult* becomes *exultation*. Form an adjective by adding **-able**, **-ous**, **-ing**, or **-ive** to a verb. Thus, *assert* becomes *assertive*. The root of each word is given in its verb form on the left. In the spaces provided, write the appropriate noun and adjective forms of each verb. You may need to drop the final **e** for correct spelling.

Verb	Noun	Adjective
1. intimidate	_____	_____
2. oppress	_____	_____
3. condemn	_____	_____
4. abominate	_____	_____

Now write sentences for the noun form and the adjective form of each verb.

1. intimidate

Noun _____

Adjective _____

_____

2. oppress

Noun _____

Adjective _____

_____

3. condemn

Noun _____

Adjective _____

_____

4. abominate

Noun _____

Adjective _____

_____

Lord of the Flies

Name: _____

ACTIVITY 21

Theme

For each character below, write a short paragraph to answer the following three questions:

　　a. What kinds of fear did the character experience on the island?

　　b. What caused those fears?

　　c. How did the character deal with those fears?

Piggy
_____
_____
_____
_____

Ralph
_____
_____
_____
_____

The Littluns
_____
_____
_____
_____

Samneric
_____
_____
_____
_____

Jack
_____
_____
_____
_____

Write an essay to explain how fear was the most dangerous and destructive force on the island. Use the back of this page or a separate sheet of paper for your answer.

Lord of the Flies
Novel Ideas Classic © 1997, Sundance

Literary Analysis
After Chapter 12 • LEVEL 3

ACTIVITY 22

Word Meaning

You have learned many new words in this unit. Use those words to complete this crossword puzzle. The definitions of the words at the bottom of the page are the clues.

Across

2. not affected or influenced by
5. completely absorbed with interest
7. possessed or influenced by demons
9. lacking confidence in oneself
12. showing an attitude of hatred
15. making afraid
17. to be made timid or afraid
19. unwilling or unable to believe
21. inspiring a mixed feeling of fear and wonder
22. feeling or expressing anger or scorn

Down

1. hard to put up with
3. unable to speak clearly
4. showing contempt or scorn
6. bitter feelings of an enemy
8. wishing evil or harm
10. disgusting, vile
11. indecent, repulsive
12. infliction of a penalty
13. sly, secretive
14. confused or mixed up
16. cruel or savage
18. laughable because of absurdity
20. threat of harm or evil

Lord of the Flies
Novel Ideas Classic © 1997, Sundance

Vocabulary
After Chapter 12 • LEVEL 3

Name: _____

ACTIVITY 23

Sequence

Below are four sets of events from *Lord of the Flies*. Number the events in each set according to the order in which the events happened. One event in each set is already numbered for you.

Set I ____

___1___ Ralph meets Piggy.

_____ The boys vote for a leader.

_____ They find a conch.

_____ Jack, Ralph, and Simon set out to explore the island.

_____ A group of boys arrive, led by Jack.

_____ The boys find a piglet but don't kill it.

_____ Ralph blows the conch.

Set II ____

_____ Piggy is knocked off the cliff by a rock.

_____ Ralph, Piggy, and Samneric go to Jack's camp.

___4___ The tribe throws spears at Ralph.

_____ The group surrounds Samneric and ties them up.

_____ Ralph calls Jack a thief.

_____ Ralph runs away.

_____ Jack and Ralph fight.

Set III ____

___6___ The boys notice that one of the littluns is missing.

_____ Everyone helps gather wood.

_____ The boys decide to light a fire on the mountain top.

_____ The fire spreads to the jungle.

_____ The boys return to the shelter.

_____ The boys dance around the fire.

_____ Flames shoot twenty feet in the air.

Set IV ____

_____ The figure lay huddled among the shattered rocks.

_____ The silver moon rose over the horizon.

_____ The twins woke up and saw the figure.

_____ A figure dropped quickly beneath a parachute.

_____ The twins ran to tell everyone that they had seen the beast.

_____ The figure landed on the mountainside.

___2___ There was a sudden bright explosion and a corkscrew trail across the sky.

On the line next to each **Set**, number the sets in the order in which they occurred in the novel.

Lord of the Flies
Novel Ideas Classic © 1997, Sundance

Reading Comprehension
After Chapter 12 • LEVEL 1

Name: _____

ACTIVITY 24

Theme

In addition to the theme of fear, there are other themes that run through *Lord of the Flies*, including:

a. There is evil in all men.

b. Democracy is only as successful as the people who make it work.

c. Manhood demands certain initiation rites.

In the spaces provided, write the letter of the theme to which each statement below applies.

____ 1. Meetings. Don't we love meetings? Every day. Twice a day. We talk.

____ 2. Jack painted his face before he went hunting.

____ 3. I got the conch . . . You let me speak!

____ 4. *Kill the beast! Cut his throat! Spill his blood!*

____ 5. This toy of voting was almost as pleasing as the conch itself.

____ 6. ____ Or else, we shall do you? See? Jack and Roger and Maurice and Robert and Bill and Piggy and Ralph. Do you. See?

____ 7. Which is better, law and rescue, or hunting and breaking things up?

____ 8. He's buzzed off . . . He's queer. He's funny.

____ 9. "I hit him," said Ralph indignantly. "I hit him with my spear. I wounded him."

____ 10. I agree with Ralph. After all, we've got to have rules and obey them . . .

Now choose any two of the symbols listed below. Write a short paragraph about each one, explaining how the symbol illustrates one or more of the themes of the novel. Use the back of this page or write your answer on a separate sheet of paper.

1. the conch

2. dazzle paint

3. the chant, *Kill the pig. Cut her throat . . .*

4. fire

5. the Lord of the Flies

6. the platform

Lord of the Flies
Novel Ideas Classic © 1997, Sundance

Literary Analysis
After Chapter 12 • LEVEL 2

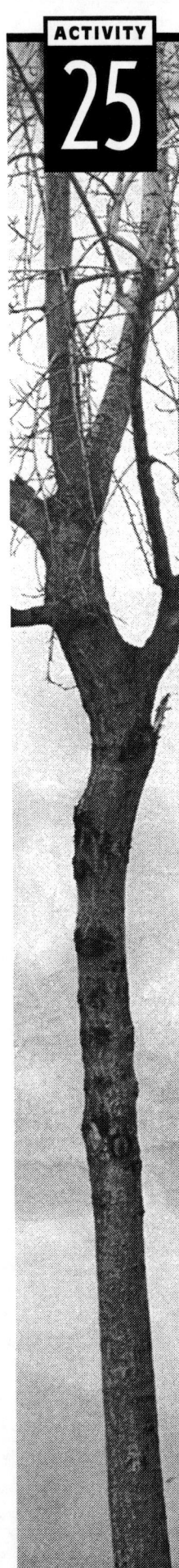

ACTIVITY 25

Characterization

Summarize each main character's attributes by answering the following questions. Use the back of this page or a separate sheet of paper for your answers.

Piggy

1. What are Piggy's greatest strengths? How are they revealed?

2. What are Piggy's greatest weaknesses? How are these weaknesses revealed?

3. Piggy is destroyed gradually. Describe the process of his destruction.

Ralph

1. After Jack invades his camp and steals Piggy's glasses, what does Ralph do? Why?

2. Why doesn't Ralph fit into Jack's new society?

3. In the end, what strengths does Ralph still possess? Why?

Jack

1. Trace the steps Jack takes to gain control of the boys on the island.

2. What techniques does Jack use to influence and control people?

3. If Jack and Ralph were to go to the same school after the rescue, how do you think Jack would treat Ralph? Why do you think so?

Lord of the Flies

Novel Ideas Classic © 1997, Sundance

Literary Analysis
After Chapter 12 • LEVEL 3

ACTIVITY 26

Characterization

According to one theory, human survival depends on the individual's ability to adapt to changes in his or her environment. In this view, only the strongest survive.

Explain how the following statement is true for each of the main characters in *Lord of the Flies*.

A person either adapts, and thus survives, or does not adapt and thus dies.

Piggy: _____
_____
_____

Simon: _____
_____
_____

Jack: _____
_____
_____

Ralph: _____
_____
_____

Using the behavior of the main characters as examples, contrast the society that Ralph created to the one that Jack created.

_____
_____
_____
_____
_____
_____
_____
_____
_____
_____
_____
_____

Lord of the Flies
Novel Ideas Classic © 1997, Sundance

Literary Analysis
After Chapter 12 • LEVEL 3

Vocabulary

I. Synonyms

Write the letter of the matching synonym in Column B for each word in Column A.

Column A

___ 1. demoniac
___ 2. diffident
___ 3. incredulous
___ 4. furtive
___ 5. truculent
___ 6. ludicrous
___ 7. enmity
___ 8. malevolent
___ 9. abominable
___ 10. oppressive
___ 11. contemptuous
___ 12. intimidated
___ 13. derisive

Column B

a. sneaky
b. hostility
c. fiendish
d. spiteful
e. threatened
f. shy
g. scornful
h. disbelieving
i. ridiculous
j. loathsome
k. ferocious
l. ridiculing
m. overbearing

II. Antonyms

Write an antonym for each of the words below.

1. enmity _____
2. malevolent _____
3. truculent _____
4. abominable _____
5. furtive _____
6. derisive _____
7. oppressive _____
8. intimidated _____
9. diffident _____
10. demoniac _____
11. incredulous _____
12. ludicrous _____
13. contemptuous _____

III. Words in Context

Choose a word from the following list to complete each sentence.

hiatus any interruption in continuity
inscrutable not able to be understood
discounted disregarded or ignored
tirade a long violent or blustering speech
glowered looked or stared angrily

1. Jack lifted his head and stared at the _____ masses of creeper that lay across the trail.

2. Piggy _____ all this learnedly as a "mirage"...

3. There came a pause, a _____ the pig continued to scream...

4. He _____ up under his eyebrows.

5. By now, they were listening to the _____

Lord of the Flies
Novel Ideas Classic © 1997, Sundance

Vocabulary
After Chapter 12 • LEVEL 2

TEST 2

Characters

I. Column A lists characters from *Lord of the Flies*. Column B contains descriptions of these characters. In the space provided, write the letter of the description next to the matching character's name.

Column A   Column B

____ 1. Piggy   a. Twins who were friendly with Ralph but who joined Jack's tribe.

____ 2. Percival   b. Boys who played in the sand and were always afraid.

____ 3. Samneric   c. Serious boy who talked to the "Lord of the Flies."

____ 4. Ralph   d. Ralph's friend, who was no leader but who had brains.

____ 5. Jack   e. Cruel boy who guarded Jack's camp at Castle Rock.

____ 6. Simon   f. Leader of the hunters who started his own tribe.

____ 7. Roger   g. A littlun who cried a lot and told the assembly about the beast.

____ 8. Littluns   h. He set the rules because the boys voted him leader.

II. Choose one of the characters listed above. Write a short account of how that character is changed by the events of the novel.

_____
_____
_____
_____
_____
_____
_____
_____
_____
_____
_____
_____
_____
_____
_____
_____
_____

Lord of the Flies   *Literary Analysis*
Novel Ideas Classic © 1997, Sundance   After Chapter 12 • LEVEL 2

TEST 3

Facts/Ideas

I. Fill in the blank with the words that best complete each statement below:

1. The conch was a symbol of _____ among the group.

2. The "Lord of the Flies" was _____.

3. The little children were afraid of _____.

4. Simon was killed by _____.

5. The boys ate mostly _____.

6. Piggy wanted a society with _____.

7. Jack and his group stole Piggy's _____.

8. _____ discovered the true identity of the beast.

9. To Simon, the *Lord of the Flies* seemed to represent _____.

10. The boys were rescued by _____.

11. The boys held their assemblies on a _____.

12. The final huge fire was set because _____.

13. _____ told Jack's tribe where Ralph was hiding.

14. Ralph called assemblies by _____.

15. Jack's group looked like savages because _____.

II. Circle the letter of the phrase that best completes each sentence.

1. The platform was located
    a. below the fort.   b. on the unfriendly side of the island.
    c. on the lower, sandy end of the island.

2. Simon suffers from
    a. strokes.   b. fainting spells.   c. whooping cough.

3. Beyond the island
    a. the world is at peace.   b. the world is at war.   c. World War III is about to begin.

4. The boys
    a. all come from the same school.   b. come from two rival schools.
    c. come from different schools and neighborhoods.

5. The island is composed of large quantities of
    a. pink granite.   b. red marble.   c. gray limestone.

Lord of the Flies
Novel Ideas Classic © 1997, Sundance

Reading Comprehension
After Chapter 12 • LEVEL 2

Name: _____

TEST 4

Facts/Ideas

I. Mark the following statements True *T* or False *F.*

____ 1. Ralph never wanted to leave the island.

____ 2. Roger was always considered an outsider by the other boys.

____ 3. Jack and Ralph were friends at first.

____ 4. Samneric were spies for Jack.

____ 5. Simon was bringing information when he was killed.

____ 6. Jack liked Piggy until Piggy began supporting Ralph.

____ 7. Jack deliberately let the fire go out.

____ 8. The sandy side of the island was protected by a coral reef.

____ 9. Jack tried to teach Piggy how to hunt.

____ 10. Jack came to depend on Piggy's wise advice.

II. Below is a list of some major events in this novel. In one short paragraph for each event, describe what the results were for each event and why it was significant in the lives of the boys on the island. Use the back of this page or a separate sheet of paper for your answers.

a. The boys vote for Ralph as chief.

b. The boys let the fire go out.

c. A dead parachutist lands on the island.

d. Simon crawls into the tribal feast to tell the group about the beast.

e. Ralph and Piggy go to Castle Rock to get Piggy's spectacles.

f. Samneric join Jack's tribe.

Lord of the Flies
Novel Ideas Classic © 1997, Sundance

Reading Comprehension
After Chapter 12 • LEVEL 2

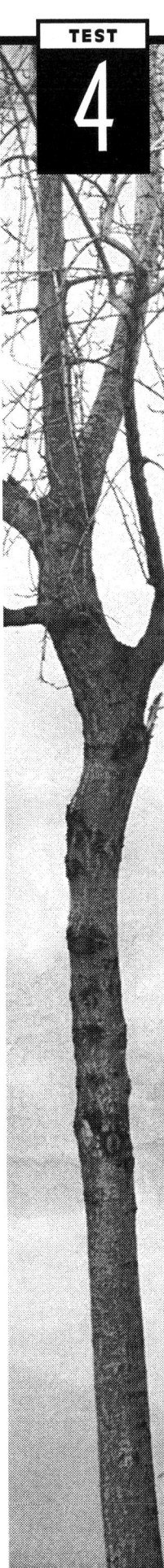

Name: _____

TEST 5

Essays

Use the back of this page or a separate sheet of paper for each answer to the following questions.

1. *Lord of the Flies* is a **parable**, a story with deep meaning, in which each of the main characters represents a different force in society. Write a brief essay analyzing the characters in terms of symbolism, concentrating on Ralph, Simon, Piggy, and Jack. Support your theories by referring to specific events in the novel.

2. When the boys are finally rescued, two of the main characters have survived (Ralph and Jack) and two have died (Simon and Piggy). In a well-organized essay, contrast the characteristics and actions of the survivors with those of the characters who do not survive.

3. As a reflection of life, what does *Lord of the Flies* suggest about the basic nature of humankind and society? Write a concise essay in which you refer to specific characters and events in the novel to support your understanding of the book's views on humanity.

4. Circle one of the words below to show how you rate *Lord of the Flies* for entertainment value.

    poor   fair   good   great

    What kind of person would most like this book?

    Write a book review of *Lord of the Flies*. Write your review on a separate sheet of paper.

Lord of the Flies
Novel Ideas Classic © 1997, Sundance

Answer Key

Activity 1
Word Meaning: Leadership

1. Answers will vary but should include personal qualities each student finds appropriate. Students should be able to explain the reasons for their rank orders. 2. Students should be able to tell why they selected the leaders they named. 3. Answers will vary but again, students should justify their choices.

Activity 2
Reading Guide: Chapters 1–3

1. deserted island in Pacific: trees, sand, beach, mountain, jungle 2. Mysteriously, their plane was shot down; the crash kills all the adults. 3. doesn't yet realize his capacity for violence. 4. Ralph; the boys feel he can set rules and give directions; he has the conch. 5. He alone can speak. 6. Afraid; this is the first indication of fear. 7. build a large fire so that a passing ship could see the smoke. 8. The boys use Piggy's spectacles as a magnifying glass to start fires. 9. He forgot to get the names of the boys. 10. Answers will vary but students should justify their choices. 11. They were concerned about different things; neither could give in.

Activity 3
Characterization

Ralph *Pros:* organized, intelligent, rational, handsome, ethical; *Cons:* too rule-oriented, places too much emphasis on order; *Reasons:* Reasons will vary. **Sample responses:** I would vote for Ralph because I trust him. He was a good leader on the island; I would not vote for Ralph because he would not make any compromises to get something accomplished.

Jack *Pros:* tall, strong, aggressive, inspires fear; *Cons:* ugly, mean, arrogant; *Reasons:* Reasons will vary. **Sample responses:** I would vote for him because I want a leader to be brave, as he was on the island; I would not vote for Jack because he was cruel to the other boys on the island.

Piggy *Pros:* intelligent, rational, logical, analytic, precocious; *Cons:* asthma, weak, boring, fearful; *Reasons:* Responses will vary. **Sample responses:** I would vote for him because he knows how to use his brains, as he showed when he suggested that they move the fire down to the beach. I would not vote for him because he is not forceful enough. He let Jack persecute him.

Write-in candidates will vary, but answers should reflect thoughtful evaluation of the character. **Sample response:** I would vote for Simon because he was a visionary. He brought information down from the mountain.

Activity 4
Cause and Effect (Literal)

1. b 2. a 3. c 4. a 5. b 6. c 7. b 8. a 9. c 10. c

Activity 5
Characterization (Literal/Inferential)

Piggy: 1. *physically:* fat, has asthma, wears glasses; *intellectually:* intelligent, rational, a thinker; *socially:* boring, afraid, wants to be liked but isn't **2.** call him "Piggy," deride him, Jack hates him; Ralph befriends him eventually.

Ralph: 1. *physically:* strong, athletic, good-looking; *intellectually:* fairly smart, thinks but needs encouragement; *socially:* friendly, congenial, diplomatic **2.** Most give in to his apparent leadership ability; Jack holds back, waiting for his chance to take power.

Jack: 1. tall, strong, freckled, red hair, ugly **2.** He's arrogant; rests on past achievements. **3.** Ralph is wary; Piggy doesn't like him; some of the others—especially the choir—follow him.

Responses will vary but students should demonstrate knowledge and appreciation of their chosen character. *For example,* some students will choose Ralph because he is smart, strong, and diplomatic.

Activity 6
Cause and Effect (Critical)

Goals and their order will vary but may include answers such as **1.** shelter **2.** fire **3.** food *Reasons will vary.* Students may find shelter more important than food. *Responses will vary.* Students may say that to build a shelter they will gather branches.

Activity 7
Reading Guide: Chapters 4–6

1. Camouflage—but it indicates a reversion to savagery. **2.** The fire had gone out. **3.** He decided hunting was more important and more interesting. **4.** He's afraid all the time. **5.** a dead paratrooper or pilot. **6.** to motivate themselves so they can kill a pig; it becomes a ritual. **7.** No. The author told us what it was, but the boys don't know that. **8.** He doesn't seem to want to be; he's having fun on a great adventure.

Activity 8
Point of View

Answers will vary. **Sample responses:** *Jack* would be shocked by Ralph's anger, then angry himself; *Ralph* would be angry with everyone; *Piggy* would be on Jack's side; *Roger* would be on Jack's side, perhaps amused by the confrontation.

Activity 9
Mood

Mood: carefree, happy, restful **Words:** *slow swing; pleasures: bright sun; whelming sea, sweet air; play good; life full of hope; floods of light; smoothed colors; pearl and opalescence; lying in the shade; sleeping*

Answers will vary. Students may choose to create a mood that is threatening, soothing, unsettled, or agitated. The words they select should support the mood they have chosen.

Activity 10
Characterization (Inferential)

Piggy: 1. He's analytical; he looks for logical answers. **2.** *Sample response:* "We know what goes on and if there is something wrong, there's someone to put it right." (Chapter 2). **Ralph: 1.** He wants to find logical explanations for things so that he does not have to worry about them. **2.** *Sample response:* "You were asleep. There wasn't anyone there. How could anyone be wandering about in a forest at night?" (Chapter 5) **Jack: 1.** hunting **2.** single-minded; physical **3.** He's afraid; he's not as fearless as he tries to make the others believe. *Answers will vary.* Some students may choose Jack because he understands his own violence and the power he exerts over others.

Activity 11
Words in Context

1. incomprehension **2.** inarticulate **3.** ludicrous **4.** embroiled **5.** charitable **6.** sinewy **7.** awesome **8.** diffident Sentences will vary but should reflect the correct usage of the word. **Sample response:** Piggy was often inarticulate.

Activity 12
Critical Reading

Ralph: *Personal qualities:* leadership; thoughtful; concerned for the group's welfare; concerned with the future; thought about rescue; sensible; logical. *Qualities of his society:* has planned rules for survival; democracy through assembly; tries to achieve consensus; cares for littluns; works toward specific goals.

Jack: *Personal qualities:* strong; impulsive; aggressive; loves to hunt; moody; hostile; cruel; manipulative. *Qualities of his society:* concern for immediate future; breaks rather than builds things; hostile and war-like; hunting and killing major concerns; dictatorial; intimidating

Answers will vary. **Sample response:** Jack's society will dominate because he grows stronger and exerts more influence over the others. Ralph's desire for order and process are reflected in the democratic features of our society. Jack's tendencies toward violence and civil disorder are present in our society.

Activity 13
Reading Guide: Chapters 7–9

1. He's homesick; misses the security of an orderly environment. 2. They use Robert as a pretend pig; it's like a fertility ritual. 3. Yes. 4. He wants and needs to be the leader. 5. Hunters. That's all they want to do, and they do it. 6. systematically, like a ritual. It's their initiation. 7. It's their entrance into savagery and into manhood. 8. one end to stick in the ground, the other for the pig's head. 9. pig's head on a stick; represents the devil, Satan, evil. 10. No; Simon is thinking that. 11. No; he's epileptic; he faints when things get too rough. 12. It's a dead man on a parachute. 13. tell them that there is no beast; to quiet their fear. 14. They mistake him for the beast. 15. Answers will vary; some students may think the boys were perfectly aware they were murdering someone they considered "odd."

Activity 14
Cause and Effect (Inferential)

1. Jack hates Piggy. **Causes:** Piggy's physical appearance; his intellectual ability; rationality; idolatry of the conch; support for Ralph; interferes with Jack's fun. **Effects:** verbal ridicule; stealing his glasses; eventual killing of Piggy; destroying the conch.

2. Piggy is afraid of Jack. **Causes:** Jack's verbal abuse; Jack's arrogance; Jack's power and threats. **Effects:** Piggy supports Ralph; advises Ralph against Jack; clings to Ralph for protection; is killed.

3. Ralph thinks Simon is batty. **Causes:** Simon goes off alone; faints; Simon makes unusual statements; Simon speaks in parables. **Effects:** Ralph doesn't believe everything Simon says but is entranced by him; they never come close to each other; eventually Simon is killed.

4. Jack hates Ralph. **Causes:** Ralph is elected leader; Ralph has the conch; Ralph believes in democracy and order; Ralph chides Jack for his actions; Ralph symbolizes good. **Effects:** Jack disobeys Ralph's orders; they argue constantly; Jack forms his own group; Jack kills Simon and Piggy, and in the end tries to kill Ralph.

Activity 15
Sequence of Events (Literal)

Signal words: first; after; finally. **Paragraph:** First, Jack bent over, looking for the pig's trail. He found clues: a cracked twig and the impression of a hoof. From the woods came the quick patter of hoofs. Jack raised his right arm and hurled the spear with all his strength. The spear hit the pig between the shoulders. After being hit, the pig squealed and crashed into the forest. Jack and the other hunters followed. The hunters found the pig tangled in the creepers. The hunters surrounded the pig and stuck it with spears. Finally, the pig died.

Activity 16
Theme (Literal)

1. He is afraid of the snake-thing—he saw it in the dark. In the morning it turned into "them things like ropes in the trees . . ." It wants to eat him. 2. snakes they see during the fire; dreams; one littlun lost in the fire 3. They have nightmares; they are without parents; they fear snakes. 4. They ignore it most of the time, don't talk about the "beast." 5. They discuss it and try to find reasons for it. 6. The beast they saw. 7. He's afraid of Roger's banging the stick. He may also be afraid of what Jack said he saw on the mountain. 8. He leaves the pig's head on a stick as an offering to the beast. 9. being killed 10. He's afraid of the beasts power and that he'll die; he faints. 11. Ralph was afraid of the unknown answers. Answers will vary. **Sample response:** Ralph is not afraid at first but grows more fearful despite his best efforts to remain rational.

Activity 17
Critical Reading

Answers may vary but should reveal an imaginative understanding of Simon's experience on the mountain and include a reasonable interpretation of the beast's words. Simon heard the beast explain that the beast of violence is not a separate being but is part of each one of us.

Activity 18
Reading Guide: Chapters 10–12

1. Piggy and Samneric. 2. He uses a large boulder balanced over a ledge with a lever under it. 3. to get Piggy's glasses so they can start the fire to cook the pig. 4. try to talk Jack into giving back Piggy's glasses. 5. He is crushed by Jack's boulder device. 6. one end to stick in the ground, the other end to stick in Ralph. 7. Answers will vary. 8. No, he's still too innocent; but he does run away in fear. 9. They see the smoke and fire that the hunters set to smoke out Ralph. 10. Answers will vary but should be justified. 11. He is relieved not to be killed but sad because he realizes man is evil.

Activity 19
Antonyms

1. encouraged 2. relieving 3. benevolently
4. flattering 5. praise 6. supporting 7. admiringly
8. forthright 9. beautiful 10. lovable

Activity 20
Structural Analysis

1. intimidation, intimidating 2. oppression, oppressive 3. condemnation, condemning 4. abomination, abominable

Sentences will vary but students should write a sentence for both the noun form and the adjective form of each verb. **Sample responses:** The bully used *intimidation* to get his way. (noun) Jason walked down the street with an *intimidating* swagger. (adjective)

Activity 21
Theme

Piggy: Piggy was afraid of Jack and his hunters; of being without his glasses; of dying; of not being rescued; of being without the stabilizing influence of adults. He's never been independent, always been fat and picked on. He copes by trying to be rational and by depending on Ralph for support and leadership.

Ralph: Ralph is not fearful in the beginning; he believes that through democratic organization they can cope with problems. Eventually he comes to fear Jack's power, fears the savagery of the hunters, fears the loss of his influence, and then fears for his life. The causes are partly his inability to adjust to the savagery of the island, partly his higher values and ethics, and partly forces outside himself, namely Jack. He copes through reason but eventually becomes "flying fear."

The Littluns: Being so young, they are afraid of just about everything, but especially snakes, nightmares, and the unknown, symbolized by the beast. They are at the mercy of the cruel world around them, having little knowledge and few logical abilities or experiences of their own to draw on. They cope by crying and then ignoring the problems.

Samneric: The twins fear Jack, the power of the hunters, and the beast. Like Simon and Piggy, they try to be rational and democratic, doing their jobs as best they can. But they want to be part of everything. They give in to Ralph. They have no solid ground on either side of the social scale. They cope by going along.

Jack: Jack seems unafraid of anything, though later he does give an indication of fear of the beast and of being hunted. His fears are unspoken most of the time; he usually acts before his fears take over. Instead, he represented fear; he caused fear in others. He counteracted fear by causing it and acting before fear could dominate him.

Responses will vary. **Sample response:** It is fear that began to disrupt the meetings and distract the boys from more practical survival matters. They become more concerned with invisible forces.

Activity 22
Word Meaning

Across: **2.** impervious **5.** rapt **7.** demoniac
9. diffident **12.** contemptuously **15.** daunting
17. intimidated **19.** incredulous **21.** awesome
22. indignant

Down: **1.** oppressive **3.** inarticulate **4.** derisive
6. enmity **8.** malevolent **10.** abominable **11.** obscene
12. condemnation **13.** furtive **14.** embroiled
16. truculent **18.** ludicrous **20.** menace

Activity 23
Sequence

Set I: 1, 5, 2, 6, 4, 7, 3; Set II: 5, 1, 6, 4, 2, 7, 3;
Set III: 6, 1, 2, 5, 7, 3, 4; Set IV: 5, 1, 6, 3, 7, 4, 2

Sequence: Set I, 1; Set III, 2; Set IV, 3; Set II, 4

Activity 24
Theme

1. b **2.** c **3.** b **4.** a **5.** b **6.** a **7.** b **8.** a **9.** c **10.** b

1. order; power; authority; civilization **2.** camouflage; savagery; animalism; primitiveness **3.** tribalism; groupthought; psychological manipulation **4.** warmth; protection; signal for rescue; destruction; death **5.** evil; sin; Satan; darkness; unknown **6.** assembly; order; rules; stability; democracy

Essay responses will vary. Answers should include these representations of the symbols.

conch: represents order because whoever holds it is allowed to speak (democracy); **dazzle paint:** represents barbarism—allows the character to be drawn out (evil); **chant:** represents violence (evil); **fire:** symbol that disperses confusion and ignorance (democracy); **The Lord of the Flies:** represents the devil in man (evil); **the platform:** represents the government (democracy)

Activity 25
Characterization (Inferential/Critical)

Piggy 1. intelligence; attempts to be scientific and rational; wants to be democratic. Incidents will vary. **2.** physically fat and can't see without glasses; he is also unable to act on his own. Incidents will vary. **3.** He is first verbally abused, called Piggy, made fun of. His glasses are broken and later stolen, so he's blinded. Then he is killed. **Ralph 1.** He tries to talk to Jack, tries to be reasonable, but that doesn't work. He doesn't want to stoop to Jack's level. **2.** He's reasonable and can't compromise his moral standards. He gets caught up in Jack's society at the dance where Simon is killed, but he regrets it. **3.** He holds on to his beliefs about order and democracy because he is not capable of changing. He nearly dies because of that. **Jack 1.** He was a leader of the choir to start with. Then he organizes the hunters. He instills fear. He organizes rituals. He ultimately takes power physically and kills when necessary. **2.** When reason doesn't work, he manipulates by fear—of lack of food, of the beasts. Then he establishes rituals. Physical force is his ultimate tool. **3.** Answers will vary. **Sample response:** Jack would probably organize a gang and persecute Ralph, just as he had on the island.

Activity 26
Characterization (Inferential/Critical)

Piggy: Although the responses will vary, the essay here should note that in spite of his mental abilities, Piggy is limited by his physical ailments and his fears. Instead of evolving, he falls apart little by little until he's killed. **Simon:** Although the responses will vary, the essay here should note that Simon also has a physical ailment, epilepsy. His (mystical) ability to see more deeply than others is an asset as well as a liability for him. He evolves beyond the others by being able to discover the identity of the beast, but he is killed because he is different from all the others. Being too different does not help one survive. **Jack:** Although the responses will vary, students should point out that Jack is the key survivor because he is aggressive, physically dominant, and instills fear. He establishes rituals that control others and give them all the strength to do what they have to do. Reason and democratic ideals have no place in his world; so in the savage world, he alone dominates. **Ralph:** Although the responses will vary, the essay here should include statements about Ralph's ideals, which seem to be the most sensible way to handle things; how those ideals do not win out against someone who fights by more primitive rules (Jack); and that, except for the author's device of having the boys rescued by a passing warship, Ralph would have been killed as Piggy and Simon were. Ralph survives by luck, not by evolutionary development. Some ethical beings are spared. **Responses will vary.** Answers should reflect the differences between order and anarchy, democracy and dictatorship.

Test 1
Vocabulary

I. 1. c 2. f 3. h 4. a 5. k 6. i 7. b 8. d 9. j 10. m 11. g 12. e 13. l

II. 1. friendship 2. benevolent 3. gentle 4. lovable 5. forthright 6. flattering 7. relieving 8. encouraged 9. bold 10. angelic 11. believing 12. sensible 13. admiring

III. 1. inscrutable 2. discounted 3. hiatus 4. glowered 5. tirade

Test 2
Characters

I. 1. d 2. g 3. a 4. h 5. f 6. c 7. e 8. b

II. Answers will vary. Some students might say that Jack undergoes the most extensive transformation, into an increasingly violent and cruel character.

Test 3
Facts/Ideas

I. 1. authority, one who could speak 2. a pig's head 3. beasts, snakes, dreams 4. the group of hunters 5. fruit and pigs 6. rules; laws 7. glasses 8. Simon 9. evil; the devil 10. a navy ship; a naval officer 11. platform 12. Jack's tribe was trying to "smoke out" Ralph 13. Samneric 14. blowing the conch 15. they painted their faces

II. 1. c 2. b 3. b 4. c 5. a

Test 4
Facts/Ideas

I. 1. f 2. f 3. t 4. f 5. t 6. f 7. f 8. t 9. f 10. t

II. Answers to essays will vary, but students should be able to support their opinions with evidence from the novel. Sample responses: **a. Effect:** He pushes the boys to take more and more responsibility for the group's well being. **Significance:** It led to Jack's faction breaking off from the group. **b. Effect:** They missed an opportunity to be rescued. **Significance:** It prolonged their stay, which later led to violence. **c. Effect:** The boys thought there was a beast on the island. **Significance:** The boys become superstitious and frightened. **d. Effect:** Simon is killed. **Significance:** Jack's group moves beyond reason. **e. Effect:** Piggy is killed. **Significance:** Ralph hides from Jack's group, who are hunting him. **f. Effect:** They become the guards of Castle Rock. **Significance:** Ralph is left completely alone.

Test 5
Essays

Essay answers will vary, but should reveal students' thoughtful consideration of the novel's ideas. For example, in answer to the first essay question students might say that Simon represents society's visionaries, poets, and prophets; Ralph, the lawgivers; Jack, the violence and aggression in society; and so on. Students should support their opinions by citing incidents from the novel.